ADVANCED**ACOUSTIC** **FINGERSTYLE**GUITAR

Master Modern Acoustic Guitar Techniques With Daryl Kellie

DARYL**KELLIE**

FUNDAMENTAL**CHANGES**

Advanced Acoustic Fingerstyle Guitar

Master Modern Acoustic Guitar Techniques With Daryl Kellie

ISBN: 978-1-78933-035-9

Published by www.fundamental-changes.com

Copyright © 2018 Daryl Kellie

Edited by Tim Pettingale

www.fundamental-changes.com

Twitter: **@guitar_joseph**

Over 10,000 fans on Facebook: **FundamentalChangesInGuitar**

Instagram: **FundamentalChanges**

For over 350 Free Guitar Lessons with Videos Check Out

www.fundamental-changes.com

Contents

Other Books by Fundamental Changes

Introduction

Through the growth of online platforms such as YouTube and Instagram, many guitarists who play "niche" styles – or who are exponents of more esoteric techniques – have gained the sort of attention previously reserved for more mainstream guitar players. One niche that has seen considerable growth due to online exposure is modern acoustic fingerstyle guitar. Due to its highly visual, flamboyant nature, it is as intriguing to watch and hear as it is entertaining.

"Modern acoustic fingerstyle" is a multi-faceted approach to playing guitar, and in this book I use the phrase as a blanket term for what is ostensibly a huge chunk of the modern guitar landscape. It includes everything from the "Travis picking" and "harp harmonics" of players like Tommy Emmanuel, to the custom tunings and percussive playing of Michael Hedges. This book is intended to introduce intermediate to advanced level guitarists to the most important techniques and concepts that are widely used in the genre, and give them complete performance pieces to develop their repertoire. If you are encountering this style for the first time, you'll find many insights into how to play the various techniques.

I remember the first time I heard Jon Gomm and Andy Mckee. I was completely astounded, both by their technical facility and their depth of emotion and expression. I was a fairly proficient fingerstyle player, having studied classical guitar in my teens, and having dipped into arranging jazz standards. But the playing of these guys was, well … from another planet!

There was no authoritative book on those techniques for me to learn from at the time, so I picked up what I could by strategically pausing video footage and pestering my favourite players for technical pointers. Over a decade later, my hope is that this book will help you engage with this style and make your learning process more efficient and accessible.

This book has been written around several technical studies, each pertaining to a specific technique, and which grow in complexity as the book progresses. Each chapter contains many smaller examples, either taken directly from these pieces in the form of "performance notes" or, they are simply exercises to help you develop the necessary technical facility to play the study piece. At the end of each chapter, you will find the notation for the full piece and there is a performance video accompanying each one.

I hope you find learning these techniques and concepts as fun and rewarding as I have.

Good luck!

Daryl

December 2018

Get the Audio

The audio files for this book are available to download for free from **www.fundamental-changes.com.** The link is in the top right-hand corner. Simply select this book title from the drop-down menu and follow the instructions to get the audio.

We recommend that you download the files directly to your computer, not to your tablet, and extract them there before adding them to your media library. You can then put them on your tablet, iPod or burn them to CD. On the download page there is a help PDF and we also provide technical support via the contact form.

For over 350 free guitar lessons with videos check out:

www.fundamental-changes.com

Twitter: **@guitar_joseph**

Over 10,000 fans on Facebook: **FundamentalChangesInGuitar**

Instagram: **FundamentalChanges**

Get the Video

*There are **15 videos** accompanying this book!*

Every study piece is played in full, so you can see exactly how it should be performed. In addition, many of the examples that demonstrate special techniques have accompanying videos to help you nail them quickly and easily.

All the videos can be found on the Fundamental Changes website by following this link:

http://geni.us/acousticvids

Chapter 1: Developing the Right Hand

One of the biggest hurdles for players who approach acoustic fingerstyle from an electric guitar background tends to be the development of their right-hand technique. Electric guitar players are often more comfortable using a pick, so fingerpicking is their most immediate obstacle. There are, of course, whole books dedicated to this technique, so the thrust of this chapter is to communicate the *essentials* to players who are crossing over to this style, and to help develop the thumb and finger independence you'll need to progress.

To get started fingerpicking, the position of the arm and hand is an important consideration.

Rest your forearm just below the elbow on the lower bout of the guitar body.

Allow your wrist to curve slightly, so you can touch the strings with your fingers.

Avoid anchoring your hand or fingers on the guitar body. (There are situations and techniques that would require this, but for this chapter the only point of contact your hand should have is the strings).

Here are a few simple exercises to help develop coordination and independence in the digits of the picking hand.

In Example 1a, each string is assigned a different picking finger.

- The thumb (**p**) picks the sixth string

- The index finger (**i**) picks the third string

- The middle finger (**m**) picks the second string

- and the ring finger (**a**) picks the first string

Play these examples at around 60 beats per minute (bpm) to begin with. It's always better to begin slowly and play accurately, before you increase the tempo. Once you are comfortable with the exercise, gradually increase the tempo at increments of no more than 5bpm after every 10 repeats of the exercise.

Example 1a is a simple picking pattern on an E minor chord. Hold the chord throughout (and do the same for examples 1b to 1e).

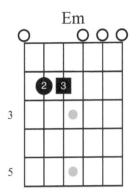

Example 1a

Example 1b expands on the previous exercise by adding a changing bass note. Use only your thumb to play these bass notes, while ensuring that strings 3, 2 and 1 are picked with the **i**, **m** and **a** fingers respectively. The correct picking pattern is included in the notation.

Example 1b

In Example 1c you will need to alternate rapidly between thumb and fingers. Take care that you don't allow the same finger to play notes on adjacent strings. As with Example 1b, the only digit to alter its position should be your thumb (**p**).

Example 1c

In Example 1d use the index (**i**) and ring (**a**) fingers to swap between strings. They should be paired and move parallel to each other, maintaining a one-string gap. Meanwhile, the thumb alternates between the low strings to form a bassline in the gaps.

Notice that the same note is played consecutively (E on the fourth string, second fret) but picked with two different digits (**i** then **p**).

Example 1d

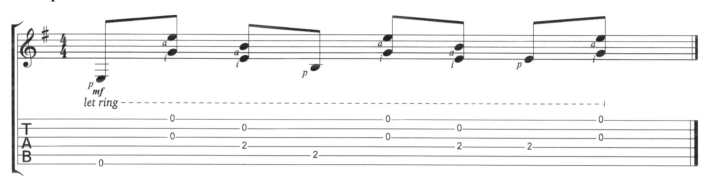

Tremolo technique is frequently used by classical guitarists and is a valuable weapon in the arsenal of the modern fingerstyle guitarist. Tremolo builds a distinctive texture from a seemingly endless flow of notes on just one string, while keeping the other strings free for basslines, melodies and chord work. In Exercise 1e, the third (**a**), second (**m**) and first (**i**) fingers are all used on the same string. This is what makes the rapid repetition of the same note possible.

It can take a few attempts to master this, especially at speed. You may find it necessary to alter the position of the hand slightly to allow each finger equal access to the string. A slight tilt in a clockwise direction should do the trick. Once you have an even sound from the notes on the second string, add in the varied bassline with the thumb.

Example 1e

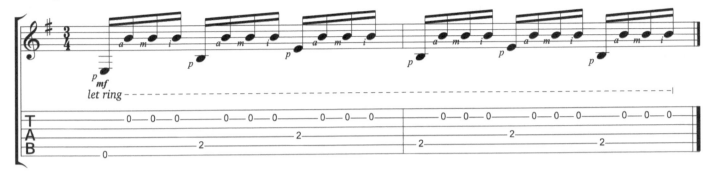

Thumb and Finger Independence

When you have got to grips with the previous examples, your right-hand coordination should be proficient enough to attempt an independent bassline played with the thumb, combined with some blues licks played on the higher strings with the fingers. The following examples break down the skills needed to play the fingerstyle piece *Riverside Blues* at the end of this chapter.

Example 1f introduces *contrary motion.* This is a device where one line ascends while another descends. In this case the bassline is ascends while the melody descends. I suggest you learn the melody part first, then add the bassline when you're confident.

Use your fingers to pick the notes on the first and second strings and your thumb to play the ascending bassline on the low strings. Treat each beat as a different chord shape. On beat 1 use your fourth finger on the 5th fret and a logical fingering for the following descending notes.

In bar two, use the nail of your index finger for the strum.

Finally, remove all your left-hand fingers except for the second finger on the fifth string, and use the index finger for the hammer-on. Listen to the audio example to hear how it should sound.

Example 1f

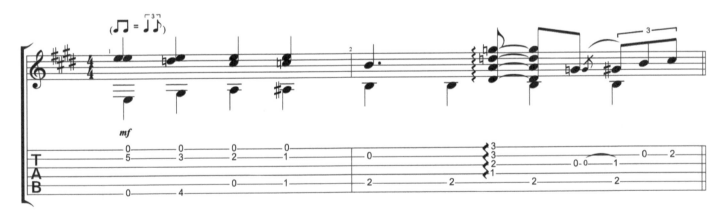

Once you have mastered this intro, study the bassline in Example 1g (played with the right-hand thumb) before learning the blues licks in Example 1h. You will combine the licks and bassline in Example 1i.

Example 1g

Example 1h

Now let's combine both parts. Playing them simultaneously may be challenging at first. Looking to see where the bass and melody parts line up in relation to each other in the notation will help you to coordinate the parts. Play very slowly to begin with.

Notes picked with the thumb have their tails pointing down, and those picked with fingers have their tails pointing up.

The stabs occur mainly in the gaps between bass notes. This is a common "trick" in this type of blues, as it creates the illusion of a thicker harmonic texture. You must occasionally jump position to play them.

There is a video demonstrating the example below to help you at

http://geni.us/acousticvids

Example 1i

Example 1j continues in the same way then adds a fill in bar two. Use the first and second fingers to play the hammer-on and pull-off.

Watch out for the occasional first finger barres (bar three, beat 2, and bar four, beats 2 and 4).

Example 1j

In Example 1k, use a logical fingering to sustain occasional chords over the moving bass notes. Watch out for the strum on beat 1 of the final bar. On beat 3, barre the index finger, but be careful not to impede the open high E string. Listen carefully to the audio example before you play it.

Example 1k

Da Coda

In the following example, use your second and fourth fingers for the sliding blues lick. This will allow you to use the first and third fingers for the bass notes.

In the final bar, on beat 1 use the left hand, first finger for the fifth string, the second for the fourth string, 6th fret, and the fourth to barre the notes on the 7th fret.

Example 11

The sliding blues lick at the start of Example 1m begins exactly like the one in bar three of the previous example, but on beat 3 use the left hand, first finger on the fifth string, the second finger on the third string, then hammer-on and pull-off with the fourth finger.

There are a few possible ways to play the phrase in bar three. Experiment until you find what's comfortable for you, but it will require some position shifts. At the end of bar three, I prefer to use the fourth finger on the 5th fret, swap around and use the middle finger for the note on the 6th fret, and finger four for the seventh fret.

Example 1m

By now, you will probably have noticed that the same voicings and fingerings are being used, but there are a couple of things to look out for. When playing the next example, watch for the sliding 6ths in bar three. Use your fourth and third fingers, then swap to first and third on the 3rd and 4th frets, with the second finger fretting the bass note.

Example 1n

Use the right hand thumbnail for the strum in bar two of Example 1o.

Example 1o

Example 1p looks tricky at first, but all the bass notes fall on the beat and the melodic line is simple triplets or swung quavers.

The bassline in bar four is fretted with the left hand thumb over the top of the neck (for the notes on the 2nd and 3rd frets). This is to facilitate the string bends.

Example 1p

In this final example, there are some more left hand "thumb" bass notes (bar one, beat 2, 3rd fret), and the occasional "pre-bend" (bar two, beat 1, and in bar one of the Coda).

In bar two of the Coda, play the 12th fret note with your fourth finger and use your second finger to reach over to the 11th fret in the bass. Simultaneously play a pull-off on the second string from the 11th to 10th fret. Practise this movement slowly to begin with and don't forget to listen to the accompanying audio,

Finally, in bar forty, use the first and second fingers on beat 4 for the first and third string, then hammer-on and pull-off with the left hand, third finger. Land the index finger on the fifth string, 2nd fret for the octave and slide up to the 12th fret for the E13 chord to finish.

Example 1q

Once you are comfortable with the previous examples, you should be ready to tackle the full *Riverside Blues* piece. I have recorded a video of the full piece for you at **http://geni.us/acousticvids**

Riverside Blues

Da Coda

Chapter 2. DADGAD Tuning

Many players of modern acoustic guitar style experiment with alternate tunings to create news sounds and textures, and DADGAD is one of the most popular.

DADGAD came to prominence through folk guitarists such as Davey Graham and Bert Jansch in the 1960s, and has subsequently become a mainstay of Celtic guitarists and modern fingerstylists alike. The sixth (low E), second (B) and first strings (high E) are all tuned down a tone, making the notes of the open strings form a Dsus4 chord.

Those new to altered tunings may find the idea of leaving the familiar, standard tuning fret map behind daunting at first. However, you'll soon realise that DADGAD tuning lends itself incredibly well to moveable chord shapes. Open string drones occur naturally and it is easy to play simple yet resonant, symmetrical chord shapes.

Example 2a illustrates a chord progression with some useful chord voicings in DADGAD tuning.

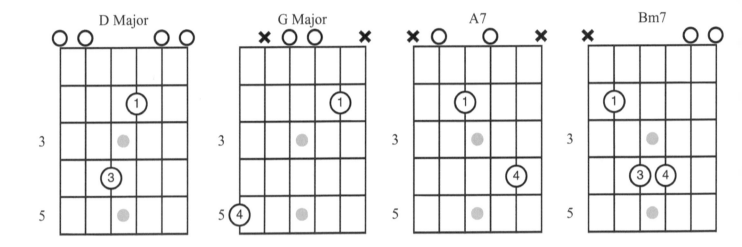

Example 2a

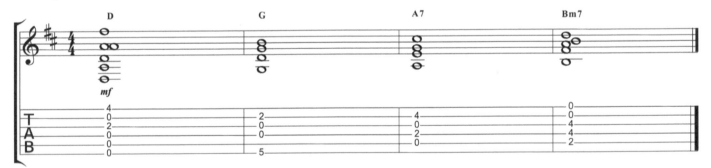

Now, here is that same sequence played as a fingerpicked broken chord pattern, with a couple of pull-offs and hammer-ons reminiscent of DADGAD players like Pierre Bensusan.

Example 2b

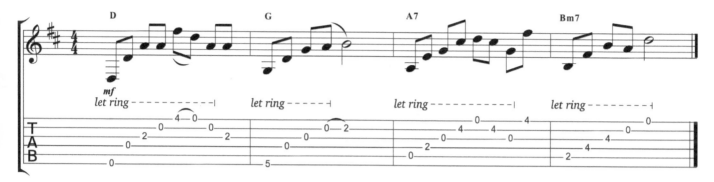

The next exercise is designed to help familiarise you with the DADGAD tuning layout by playing the D Major scale. Notice how the tuning facilitates the use of sustained open strings. Be sure to let the notes ring into each other for maximum effect.

NB: Examples 2c and 2d have accompanying videos to help you at ***http://geni.us/acousticvids***

Example 2c

The next few examples relate to one of two DADGAD practice tunes I've included for you. The first is a version of the traditional Irish jig, *The Blackthorn Stick*, arranged for DADGAD. Work through the following excerpts to master the techniques before tackling the full piece.

In Example 2d, for the entire first bar, the first finger is anchored on the third string, 6th fret, and the fourth finger is anchored on the fourth string, 9th fret (in much the same way as you hold down a chord shape). This type of *anchoring* allows the notes to continue to ring into each other.

The necessary right hand fingering (**p, i, m, a**) is written in for the first few bars. For the arpeggiated chord in bar four, quickly unfurl your right hand **p, i** and **m** fingers, staggering the timing of the picking slightly.

Example 2d

Use the first finger to play the *glissando* in bar seven of Example 2e. Next, pull off the left hand index finger to the open string and pick the open strings that follow with alternating right hand fingers (**i** and **m**). Continue to alternate the picking fingers to play the same notes in bars nine and ten (the fingering is labelled).

Example 2e

For the concluding passage, remember to alternate the right hand picking fingers for the open strings at the end, as in the previous example.

Example 2f

Now have a listen to the full arrangement of *The Blackthorn Stick* and watch the video at **http://geni.us/ acousticvids** before tackling the piece.

Remember to play it slowly and accurately to begin with.

The Blackthorn Stick

Now that you are a bit more familiar with DADGAD tuning, here is a more challenging arrangement. Once again, we will look at some excerpts from the tune to focus on the required technique and fingering.

In bars one to four, only two chord shapes are used. For the first shape, barre your first finger across the 4th fret. Fret the note on the sixth string with your second finger. Use your third finger to play the note on the second string.

In bar five there is an arpeggiated chord. Play this using the same approach as Example 2e. In bar five, beat 3, use your left hand fourth finger to reach up to the 7th fret, while keeping the rest of the chord held down.

Example 2g

The new voicing in bar seventeen can be a bit challenging. Hold this chord down using the second finger to fret the bass note on the sixth string, the third finger on the second string, the fourth finger on the first string, and the first finger on the third string.

Example 2h

To play the chord shape in bar eighteen you'll need to make a bit of a stretch. Use your first finger to hold down the bass note. Use your second finger on the third string, third finger on the first string, and fourth finger on the second string.

Watch out for the pull-off in bar twenty-six (use the fourth finger for this).

In bar twenty-seven, barre your first finger across the top three at the 2nd fret. Add your second and third fingers to play the notes on the 3rd fret, then play the 5th fret note with your fourth finger while still holding down the chord.

Example 2i

In bar thirty-five, use the first finger to fret the sixth string, the fourth finger for the second string, and the second finger for the third string.

Maintain this shape, but don't block the first or fifth strings – they are needed for an open string and a harmonic. Hold the tip of the index finger over the 7th fret and pick with either the thumb or third finger nail).

Use the third finger on string four in the next bar.

Example 2j

The second time ending to the tune uses some rather dark (and at times discordant) minor sounds.

In bar forty-one, beat 2, fret these notes using the second and third fingers, and use the fourth finger to play the first string, 3rd fret.

In bar forty-two, beat 1, use the first and third fingers. On beat 2 use the second finger, then the fourth finger on beat 4.

In bar forty-three, beat 1, use the first and second fingers. For beat 2 use the third finger, and on beat 3 the fourth finger.

Example 2k

Watch the performance video at **http://geni.us/acousticvids** before tackling the study piece.

Gymnopédie No.1

Chapter 3. Travis Picking

"Travis picking" is one of the most prominent techniques used in fingerstyle guitar and is named after legendary country guitarist Merle Travis. The technique is achieved by playing alternating strings with the thumb to produce a bassline and/or chord accompaniment, while the fingers play a melody on the higher strings.

Originally a Country and Folk mainstay, the technique has since been used by everyone from Tommy Emmanuel and Doyle Dykes to Paul Simon and Lindsay Buckingham.

The examples given here are written in standard tuning and assume the use of a thumb pick, like Merle Travis and Chet Atkins would have used. If you don't have one, or just prefer to use your bare thumb, that's fine too.

Example 3a will help you get going with this technique. Pick this pattern on simple C and G chords, but be sure to use *only your thumb*. You should also "palm-mute" the low strings slightly by resting your right-hand near to the bridge.

Example 3a

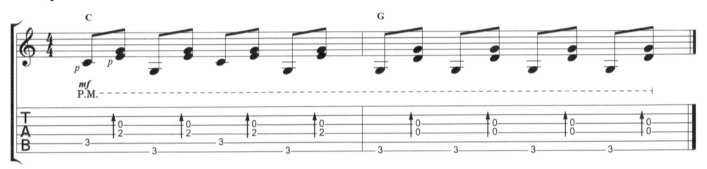

Now learn this melody played on the high strings.

Example 3b

Now join the two parts together! Watch the video of Example 3c at **http://geni.us/acousticvids** to get some more insight.

The melody is played with the fingers, while the thumb takes care of the accompaniment.

Example 3c

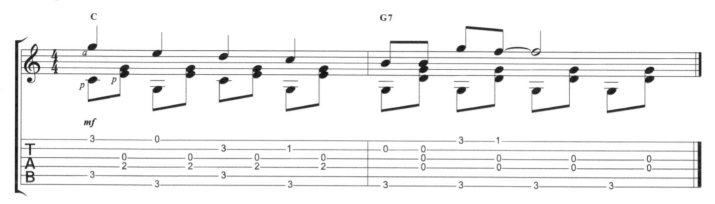

If you're not used to playing this style, it can seem a little overwhelming at first. My advice is to look at the thumb part first and see where the melody notes line up with the bass notes. Treat these as one movement of your fingers.

For example, on beat one of the first bar, the bass note (picked with your thumb **p**), and the melody note (picked with your ring finger **a**) are played simultaneously. Practise this movement until it is smooth, then add the next part of the phrase – in this case the two middle strings picked simultaneously using only the thumb.

(If in doubt, remember that notes picked with the thumb always have the stems pointing down and those picked with the fingers have the stems pointing up).

Bear in mind that the strings with the melody on should not be palm muted, even though the lower strings are. This requires you so angle your picking hand slightly, but it will achieve the effect of creating a solid rhythm part, while the melody rings our clearly.

Example 3d

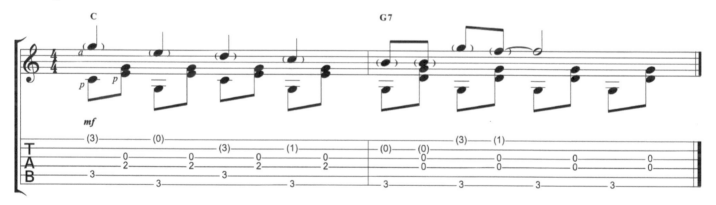

Once you have the hang of the basic Travis pattern, try this more complex one, based loosely on the picking in *Cannonball Rag* by Merle Travis.

Example 3e

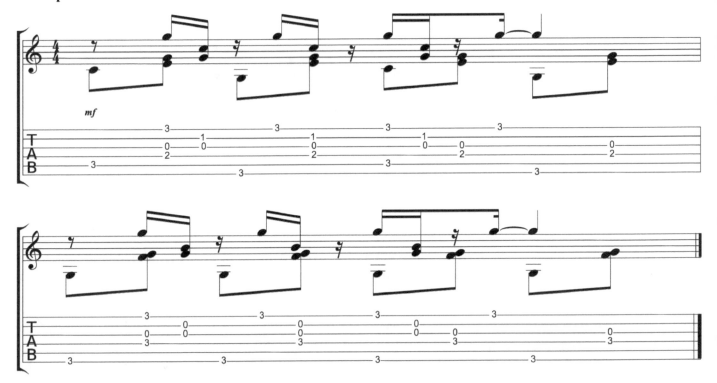

As with the previous examples, begin by identifying the points at which the thumb and finger parts line up and practise those individual movements. In this example you will also be required to occasionally pick pairs of strings.

Example 3f

Further Techniques

We have covered some of the basics of Travis picking but of course there have been many players who have expanded upon this technique and added ideas of their own.

Here are some examples of the banjo-inspired style of Jerry Reed. We will learn a full-length piece called *Jerry's Roadside Assistance*, later but let's first look at some parts in greater detail.

In Example 3g you will play a melodic line which combines open strings and pull-offs.

Begin by using your first finger to barre the 5th fret and use the third finger to play the hammer-on and pull-off. The next note on the fourth string should be picked with the thumb.

The double-stops in this example are always picked with the first and second fingers and the following notes (usually on the fourth string) are picked with the thumb.

Examples 3g and 3h are demonstrated for you in videos at **http://geni.us/acousticvids**

Example 3g

In Example 3h, check carefully which finger you should pick with.

This is a similar idea to the "open string scale" from the last chapter, but with some pull-offs and slides added.

Example 3h

Example 3i uses a repetitive picking pattern in the right hand:

- Thumb (**p**) picks the fourth and fifth string (and six at the very end)

- First finger (**i**) picks the third string

- Second finger (**m**) picks the second string

- Third finger (**a**) picks the first string

Example 3i

Example 3j uses a lick which features hammer-ons on the third string, followed by a jump up to the first string. Use your thumb to pick the notes on the third string and your third finger for those on the first string.

Example 3j

Here is the full study in the style of the late, great master of the thumb pick, Jerry Reed (see **http://geni.us/acousticvids** for the video).

Jerry's Roadside Assistance

Standard tuning

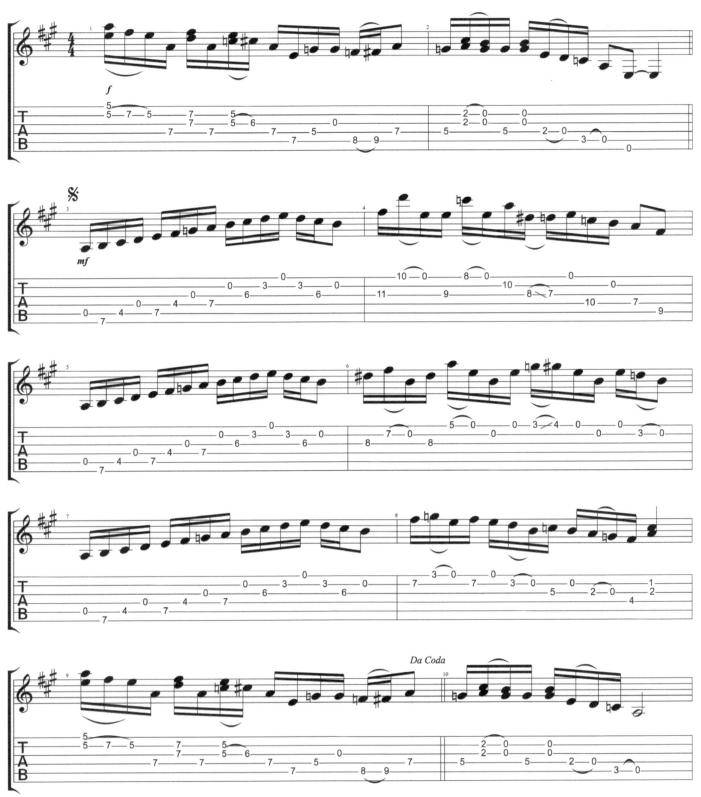

48

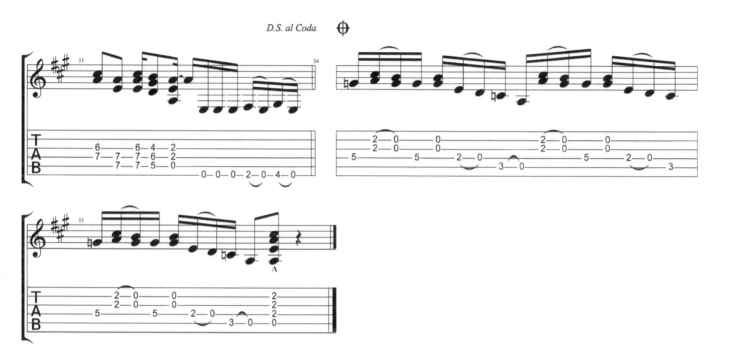

Chapter 4. Harmonics

Some musical instruments are capable of producing notes called harmonics. On a guitar, we do this by touching a string at a "node" point and then plucking the string and allowing the harmonic to ring out. The result can be used to produce a whole range of ethereal, harp-like effects. This technique also allows us to produce notes at pitches which would otherwise be impossible to play on an acoustic guitar.

To play Example 4a, gently touch a left hand finger onto the string, directly over the fret notated in the tablature. Don't use any pressure, the string shouldn't move, and it certainly shouldn't be pushed into the fret bar. Now pick the string with a right hand finger.

Remove your left hand finger just as you pick the note to allow the string to ring unhindered.

You may find it useful to play the 12th fret harmonics with your fourth finger, and the 7th fret harmonics with your first finger, to allow for the stretch between the two positions.

Notice that you can easily spot harmonics in the notation because of the "diamond" shape around them.

Examples 4a – 4d inclusive all have accompanying videos at **http://geni.us/acousticvids**

Example 4a

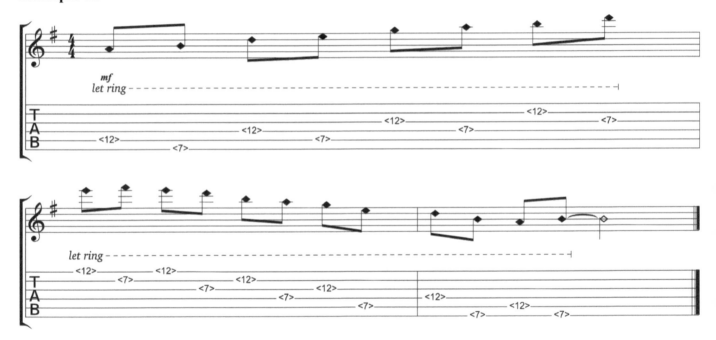

Example 4b explores this idea in drop D tuning (tune just your low E string down a tone to D). Changing the tuning of a string will shift the position of the natural harmonics.

For the rest of this chapter we will remain in drop D tuning.

Notice the change in rhythm in the second bar, although the fretted notes remain the same.

Be as accurate as possible as being even a tiny amount away from the node will hinder or prevent the harmonic from sounding.

Example 4b

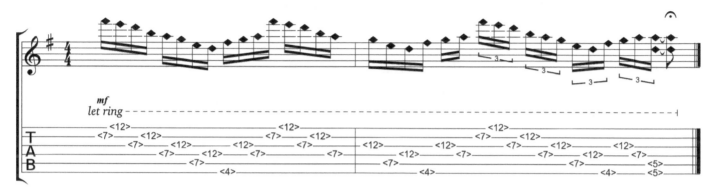

The next example uses natural harmonics to outline simple chords played on the up-beats of the bar. Barre across the 12th fret with the third finger to play them. Remember, don't push the string into the fret, touch it lightly and don't use any pressure.

Next, use the first finger to play the 7th fret to play the harmonics then slide this "barre" down to the 5th fret. Use your picking thumb and first finger to play them.

Example 4c

Example 4d is the same idea with an added percussive part. Play this by lightly slapping your thumb on the low strings in between the harmonics.

Example 4d

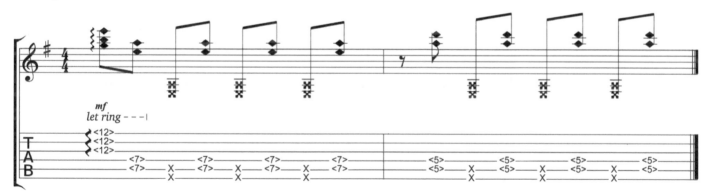

51

Here is a more complex idea that combines harmonics with a percussive part on the low strings, similar to the previous example. You may wish to leave out the percussive part initially.

Example 4e

The following examples demonstrate the technique called *tapped harmonics* which involves tapping on the fret itself, rather than picking above it.

In Example 4f, barre the 2nd fret across the bottom three strings to form an E minor chord in drop D tuning).

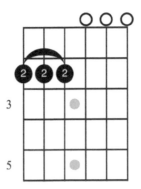

Use the middle finger to tap quickly on the 14th fret (12 frets above the fretted note). "Bounce" the tapping finger quickly and the harmonic will ring.

Continue to sound the chord by tapping 12 frets above each the fretted note. Tap the 12th fret above the open strings at the end of the example.

Practise this technique until all the harmonics ring out clearly, and you can outline the chord smoothly, allowing the notes to ring into one another.

Example 4f

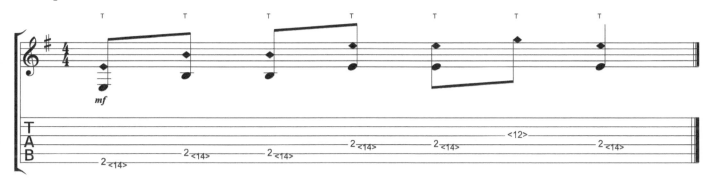

Here is a triplet idea that combines a tapped harmonic with a hammer-on.

Tap the 12th fret with the middle finger, then hammer-on the fretted notes with the first and third fingers.

Example 4g

Next, use the middle finger to tap the harmonic on the 12th fret, then hammer-on the left hand fingers to sound the remaining triplets, as in the previous example.

Notice that the third note in the triplet is a hammer-on to a different string. You may have to hammer a little harder than usual to make it sound.

The final chord uses tapped harmonics simultaneously across three strings. Tap using the underside of the index finger, keeping it parallel to the frets to let all three notes to ring.

Example 4h

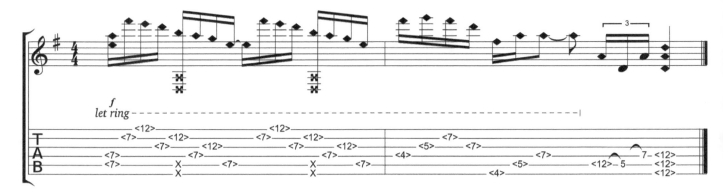

Now let's have a look at the full study which is composed almost entirely from natural harmonics.

As harmonics have a distinctive "twinkling" sound, I've named this piece *Lyra*, after the constellation. Watch the video at **http://geni.us/acousticvids**

Lyra

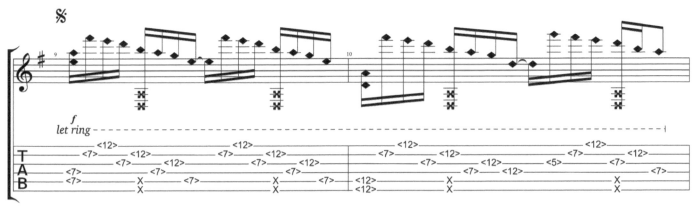

Da Coda

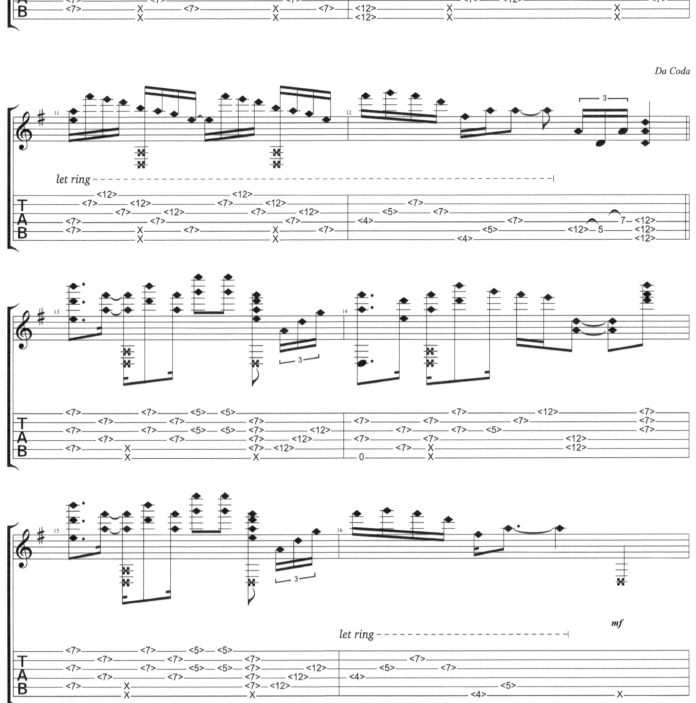

D.S. al Coda

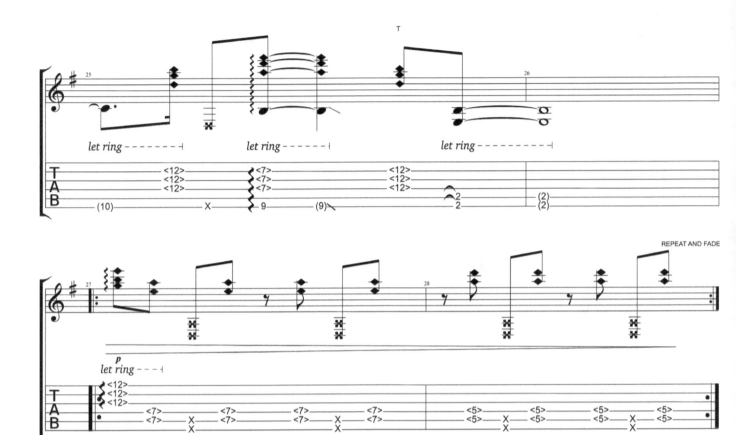

Chapter 5. Artificial Harmonics

The *natural* harmonics we covered in the previous chapter are useful for playing in keys that lend themselves to the use of open strings, but *artificial* harmonics can be used in any key. Artificial harmonics are achieved by touching the node point 12 frets above any note – whether it is an open string or a fretted note – while picking the string with the thumb as illustrated below.

Try out this technique by playing the natural harmonics at the 12th fret to begin with, but instead of using both hands, use only your picking hand.

Position the tip of the index finger over the node-point (sixth string, 12th fret, over the fret wire itself). Now use your thumbnail, or thumb pick, to pluck the string. Remember to lift the index finger slightly after picking the note to allow the harmonic to ring out.

Next, pick the open third string normally with your third finger. Continue this pattern across the fretboard as shown below. The result is a lush "harp" effect.

See it demonstrated at **http://geni.us/acousticvids**

Example 5a

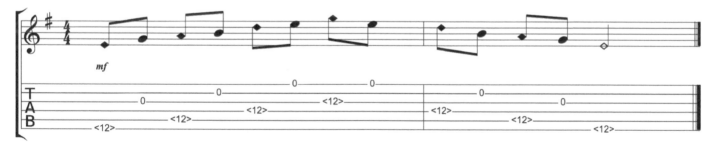

It can take a little time to achieve a smooth "cascading" effect, so practise this until it sounds consistent.

Now you have eliminated the left hand when sounding harmonics, you can use it to outline chord shapes instead. Barre the 5th fret with your first finger and use your fourth finger on the first string.

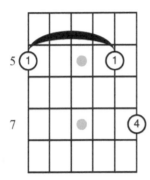

Use the same technique as in the previous example to outline the chord using a combination of regular notes and artificial harmonics. Position your index finger over the 17th fret (12 frets above the 5th fret) to play this, and check out the video to this example in action.

Example 5b

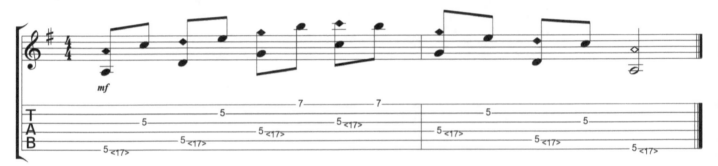

Now try these harp harmonics on a more complex chord shape. This example is taken from the study piece at the end of this chapter.

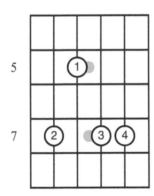

To play Example 5c, place your fingers in the chord shape above. Use the same picking technique as Example 5b to trace the outline of the chord at the 17th and 19th frets. Take this slowly and build up speed gradually. It can be challenging to coordinate your fingers at first!

Example 5c

The same principle applies to Example 5d, but this time I've added some embellishment in the form of pull-offs. The diagram below indicates the fingering you should use. The black dots are the notes that you will pull off *from* with your third finger.

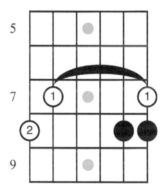

Example 5d

Some of the harmonics you will encounter in the study piece are played using the two-handed technique from the previous chapter. In Example 5e, begin by using the same technique as Example 5d. For the harmonics on beat 1 of bar two, simply lay the first finger gently across the 7th fret and pick the strings with your thumb, and first and second fingers.

This example is demonstrated in a video at **http://geni.us/acousticvids**

Example 5e

The next section of the study piece involves some swift changes between the two-handed and one-handed techniques, as demonstrated in Example 5f.

The first bar uses the harp technique almost exactly as demonstrated in Example 5a. In bar four, the first five notes are "harped" using the two-handed technique, and the second 12th fret harmonic (on the up-beat of beat 3) is also played two-handed, along with the final two notes.

Example 5f

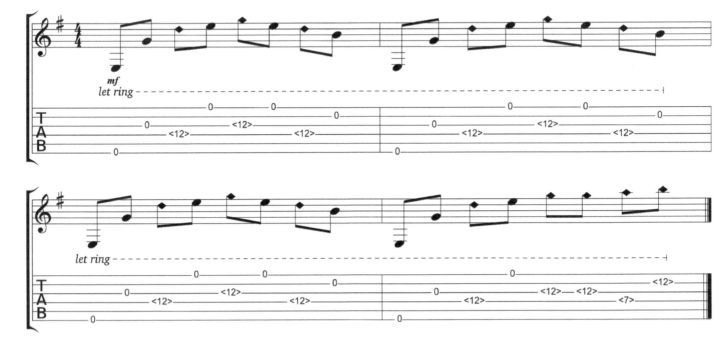

The final example demonstrates some more harmonic techniques.

The harmonic in bar thirty-six is tapped at the 12th fret (as per Example 4g).

The following harmonic is also tapped, but this time hammer-on with your left hand to the 3rd fret, then pull-off to the open string. The following open string is picked conventionally with the thumb.

In the second half of bar thirty-seven, fret the notes on the second and fourth strings, then slap the 12th fret with the middle finger. This will cause the natural harmonics of the open strings to sound, but you will also hear the other fretted notes.

In the following bar, keep the same chord shape held down with your left hand, and use a similar technique to the harp effect shown in earlier examples, however this time play the harmonic and third finger note simultaneously. These techniques are all shown in the video of the study piece at the end of the chapter.

Example 5g

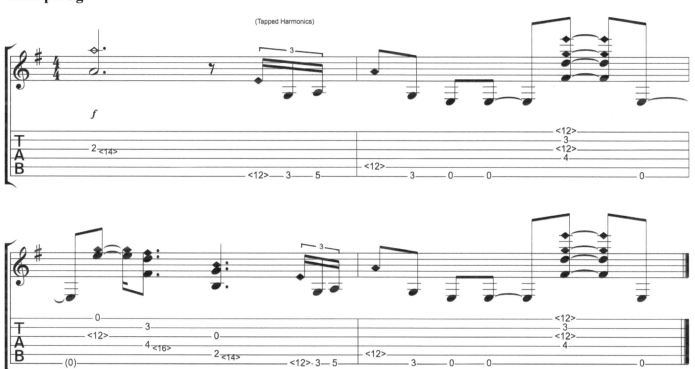

Once you are comfortable with the techniques, try the study piece, called *Snow*. This was originally written as a duet with violin and it consolidates all the harmonics techniques covered so far.

There is a performance video at **http://geni.us/acousticvids**

Snow

Standard tuning

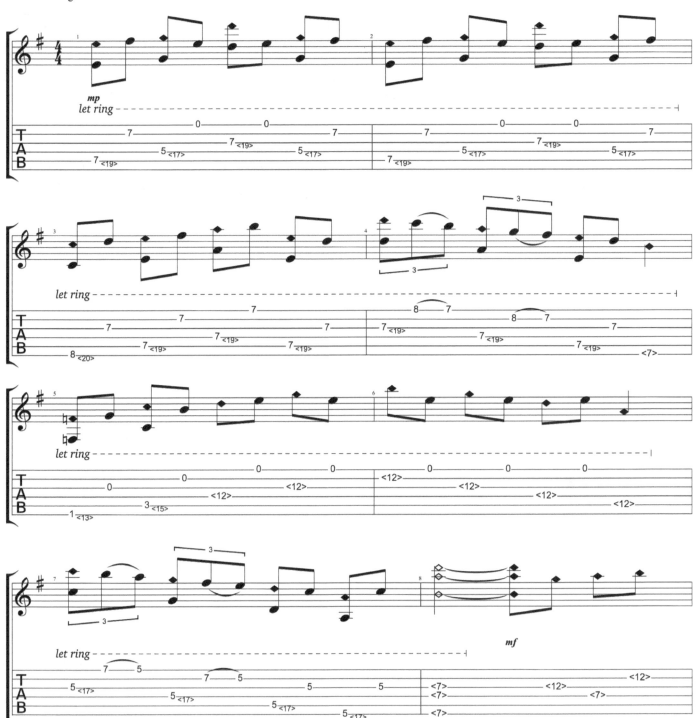

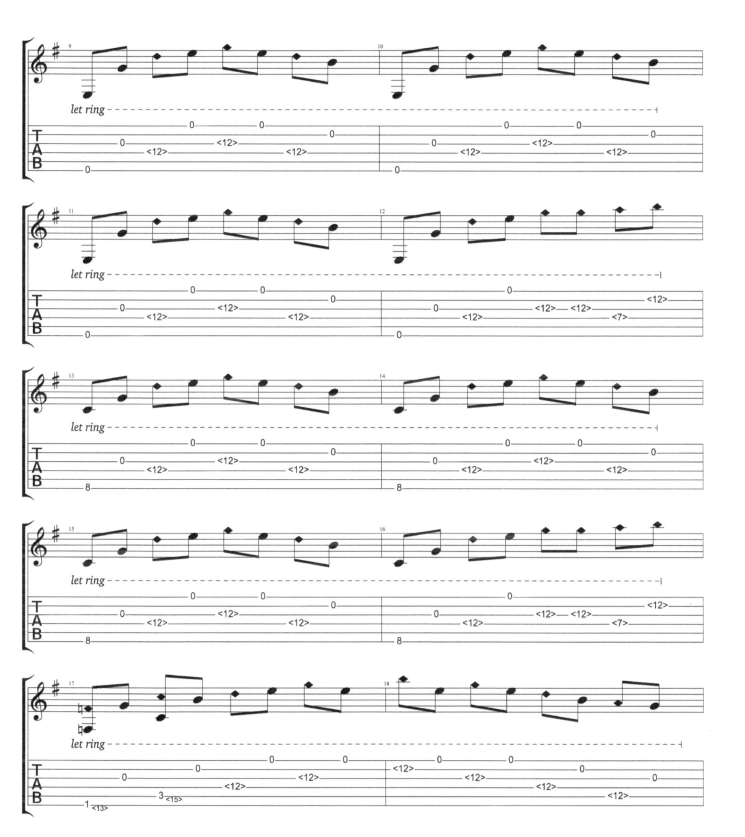

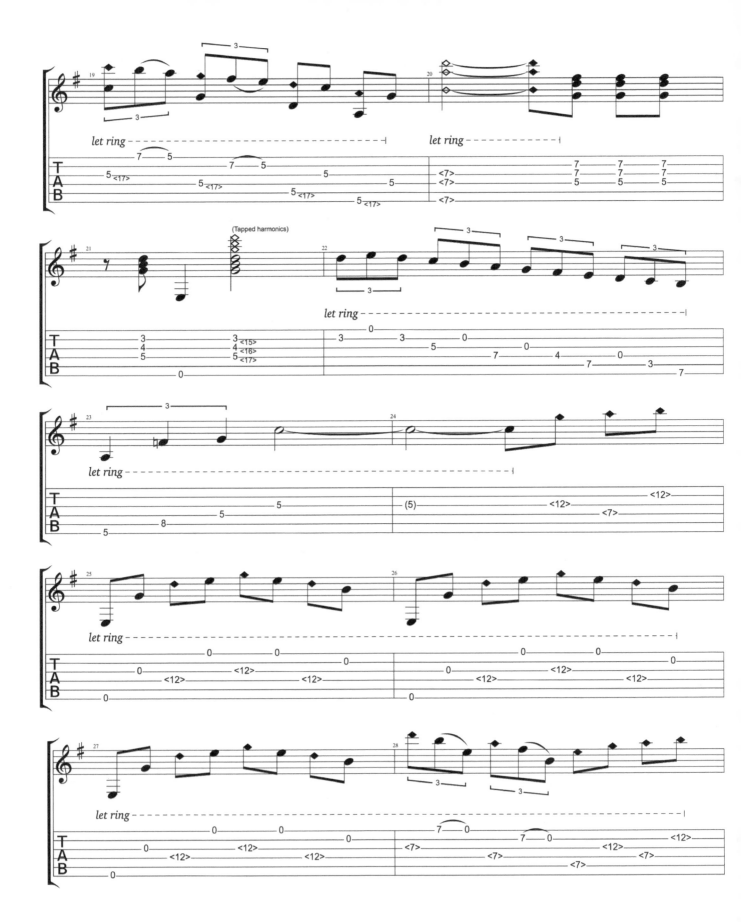

let ring

Chapter 6. Fret Tapping

Fret tapping is a technique used in several genres of guitar playing. In the context of fingerstyle acoustic, it requires the guitarist to produce a sound by hammering onto the desired notes on the fretboard, rather than plucking a string in the conventional manner – and this can be done with either hand.

As an intermediate or advanced level guitarist, you will no doubt have encountered this technique in a rock guitar context. In the contemporary acoustic setting, it is generally used in a less "linear" fashion, allowing players to achieve lush, multi-layered textures, often freeing up the hands to be able to include percussive effects and harmonics.

For this chapter you need to tune your guitar to CGDGAD. This is similar to DADGAD, but the fifth and sixth strings are tuned down a tone further.

Example 6a is designed to help you get used to tapping using only your left hand.

Begin by hammering onto the frets with your first and third fingers together. Now, pull off to the open strings. Take care not to make any other strings ring. Repeat as illustrated below until you can execute the movement smoothly. Lightly palm mute the first two bars, then gradually increase the volume in bars three and four.

Example 6a

Now, using only your *right* hand, fret-tap on the low strings to outline a simple chord progression. The diagram below shows where your hand should be positioned in relation to the fretboard.

Use your index finger to barre and hammer-on to the fifth and sixth strings. You will need to angle your hand around slightly as shown.

Now, move and hammer-on the same finger to the 2nd fret, then 4th fret, and finally pull off to allow the open strings to sound.

Example 6b

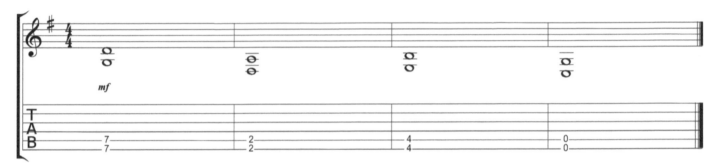

The study piece at the end of this chapter combines these two parts, so you will need to practise playing them at the same time and this is taught in Example 6c. Play through it slowly at first, paying attention to where the parts line up in the notation.

Keep the right hand index finger held down for the whole bar, while the left hand fingers bounce on and off the frets. The diagram below shows how the hands should be positioned.

Watch the video of Example 6c to see how it should be done: **http://geni.us/acousticvids**

Example 6c

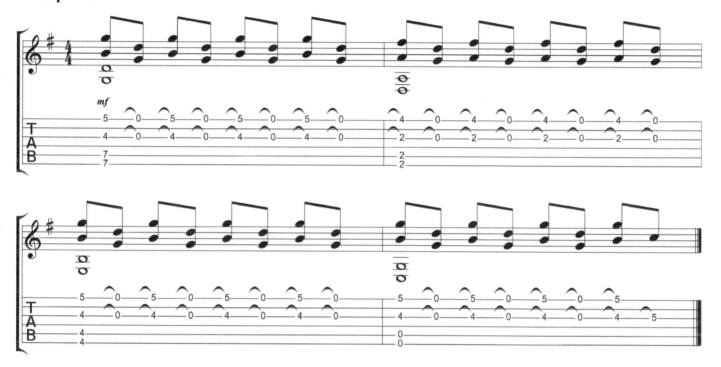

In Example 6d, all the notes on the sixth string are fret-tapped with the right hand. Begin with your index finger on the 7th fret.

Next, use your left hand, first finger, to lightly pull on the second string, causing the open string to sound, then use it to hammer-on to the 3rd fret. Next, Use your second, then third finger to play the notes that follow.

Bars three and four are similar, but use your first finger for the hammer-on.

Example 6d

The piece continues with the right hand tapping sustained bass notes while the left hand taps a melody. In twenty-two, play these harmonics conventionally with the left hand over the 5th fret and the right hand picking the strings.

Example 6e

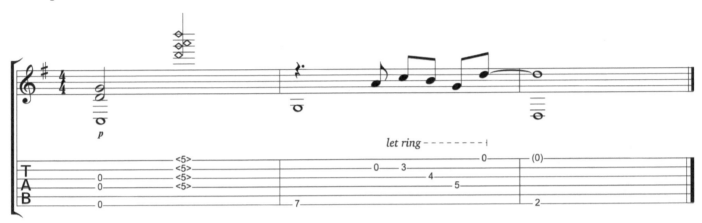

The strums (as indicated with the directional arrows in Example 6f) are played conventionally with the right hand.

Example 6f

At the start of bar thirty-one the roles of the hands swap briefly and the left hand is used on the low strings and the right for higher ones.

All the following instructions are harder describe in than simply show you, so I've created a demonstration video for Example 6g that you can find at **http://geni.us/acousticvids**

Use the second finger of the left hand to tap the sixth string, and third finger to tap the fifth string. Now tap the 4th fret with the *right hand* index finger and pick the open strings with the third and second fingers.

To play the next two notes, the right hand index finger taps the 5th fret, while the left hand moves up to tap on the sixth string with the second finger.

In bar thirty-three, pick the open stings with the right hand index finger. The high open strings that follow are played by the left hand. Pull the left hand down towards the floor to lightly catch the strings.

Example 6g

Perhaps the most challenging section of the piece occurs in bars 57-60, illustrated in Example 6h. Again, there is a video to help you understand how the piece comes together at **http://geni.us/acousticvids**

Begin by tapping the notes on the 9th fret with the right hand. The next two notes on the 5th fret are tapped with the left hand.

Follow this with a right-hand tap on the 9th fret with the first finger. The second finger will then play the open third string.

Use the left hand to play the next two notes on the 5th fret, then the right hand first and second fingers for the following notes on the 7th fret.

In bar fifty-eight, fret tap the notes on the 9th fret with the left hand fingers, then *cross over the hands*, tapping the 5th fret with the right hand first finger and the open string with the third finger.

Now, uncross the hands and tap with the first finger onto the first string, 2nd fret. Follow with the right hand second finger for the open second string.

Finally, tap the next two notes on the 5th fret with the right hand fingers, then *cross the left hand underneath the right* to tap the notes on the 7th fret with your left hand fingers.

Example 6h

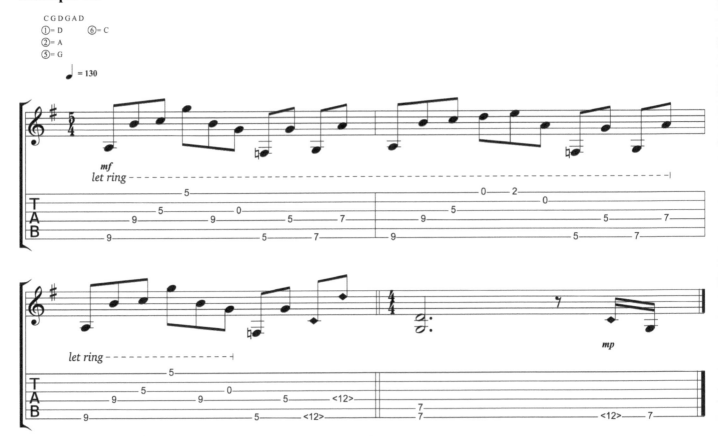

After you have taken enough time to study these isolated parts and are feeling comfortable with them, try the full fret-tapping study. Take your time and work on making everything sound clean and smooth.

Next Time Around

D.S. al Coda

Chapter 7. Percussive Effects

One of the most striking elements of modern acoustic fingerstyle playing is the use of percussive sounds, whether these are taps, slaps, thumps or scratches! There are, of course, an almost limitless number of ways to create these effects and in this chapter we will explore the most commonly used ones.

Experiment with the precise location of these percussive hits on your guitar, because every guitar will sound a little different.

In this chapter we will use another alternate tuning. It is based on the CGDGAD tuning used in the previous chapter, the only difference here is that the second string is tuned down a semitone further to Bb, producing a C G D G Bb D tuning.

All of the percussive effects in this chapter are demonstrated for you in the accompanying videos at **http:// geni.us/acousticvids**

In Example 7a, use the heel of the right hand palm to hit the guitar body near the bridge. This is notated with an X on the sixth string of the guitar tablature. The sound you are looking to achieve is a low "thud". You are using the body of the guitar like the kick drum on a drum kit.

Example 7a

In examples 7b and 7c, the sounds notated on the fifth and fourth strings respectively are created by hitting your finger tips against the guitar body near the neck and sound hole. It can be done either above or below the strings as indicated.

Example 7b

Example 7c

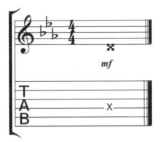

Finally, the sound notated on the third string is made by slapping the fingers against the side of the guitar, usually underneath the upper bout, or slightly further around nearer the neck (particularly if you are using your left hand to do this).

Example 7d

Each of these techniques produces a different tone and provides a different effect you can use to enhance a performance.

Before we move on to some musical examples, note that all the music in this chapter is played with an *inverted left hand* technique. This means that the left hand reaches over the top of the guitar neck, as illustrated below. You may have seen guitarists like Preston Reed, Andy Mckee and Jon Gomm use this technique.

The musical examples in this chapter are notated using four staves, with the left-hand and right-hand parts each having their own notation and tablature. Most fretted notes are tapped, so notating them in this way avoids any ambiguity over which hand to use. Plus, with all the various percussive sounds, a conventionally notated transcription would get very crowded and hard to read!

In Example 7e, begin by playing just the left-hand part. Read the instructions below and also refer to the video demonstration.

Tap with your first then second finger onto the 8th fret notes using the inverted left hand technique. Then add a percussive hit, as illustrated in Example 7c. Next, barre the left hand index finger and use it to tap both strings on the 5th fret. Pull off the barre, making the open string sound, then hammer back onto the 5th fret again. Finish with another percussive hit.

Example 7e

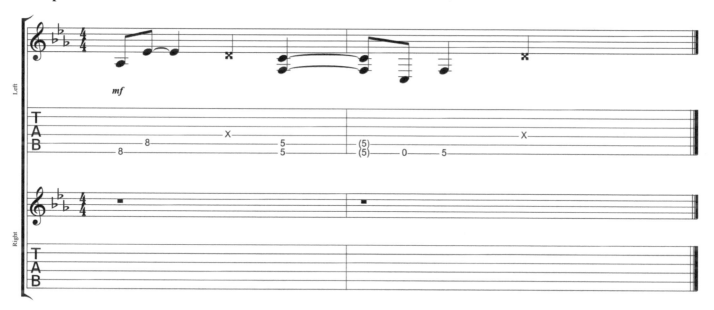

Use your right hand to play the largely percussive section in Example 7f. Begin with the "kick drum" sound with the heel of the palm (see Example 7a), followed by the fingertips on the body (Example 7b), then another "kick drum".

All of the harmonics are tapped.

The final percussive hit in bar one is a slap on the side of the guitar body.

Bar two begins the same, but doubles up the fingertip percussion and has tapped harmonics on strings four and five.

To play the final chord at the 5th fret, cross the right hand over and fret-tap strings five and six with the index finger.

Example 7f

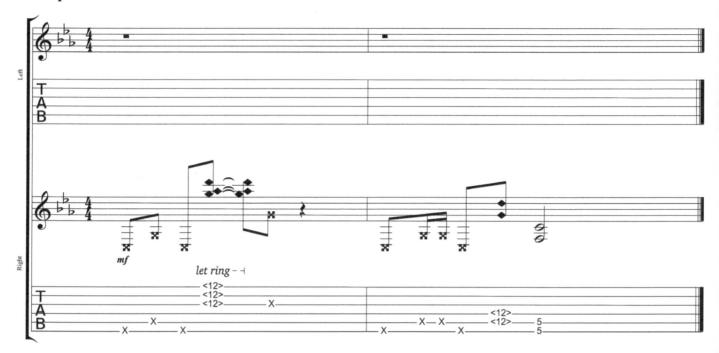

The next step is to put both hands together. Here are some tips to play Example 7g:

- Be aware of how the two parts line up with each other rhythmically.

- Notice that some notes will be played simultaneously with two hands, whereas others occur in the gaps between each other.

- The harmonics in the first bar are played conventionally (albeit using the inverted left hand position), striking the strings with the nails of the right hand.

- The percussive triplet is played by drumming the fingers (first, third and fourth) on the guitar body. The hit that follows is executed with the left hand as in Example 7c.

Example 7g

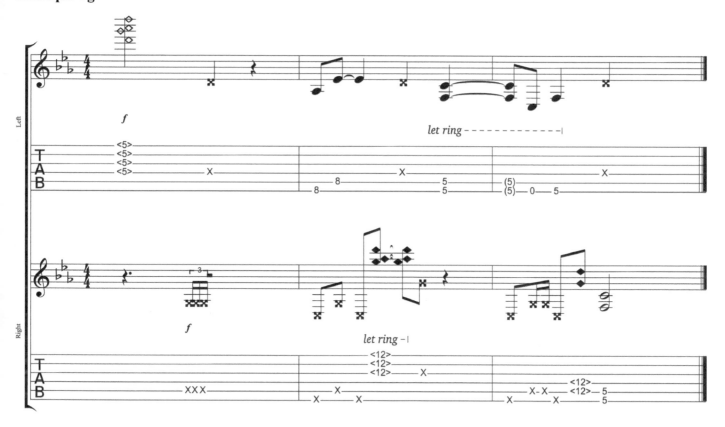

The second part of this section (Example 7h) begins with percussive hits in the right hand.

Execute a "kick drum" hit (as Example 7a), while simultaneously hammering the left hand onto the sixth string, third fret. The following pull-off coincides exactly with the next percussive hit in the right hand, followed by another "kick drum".

Tap the harmonics on the 12th fret, followed by a left hand percussive hit.

Next is a percussive hit by the right hand, after which use the right hand to barre and fret-tap the 10th fret.

In bar five, pull off the right hand barre and follow it with a series of left hand hammer-ons and pull-offs played with the first finger. Meanwhile, the right hand plays percussive hits.

Example 7h

The next section is less percussive, consisting almost entirely of two-handed fret tapping.

Example 7i

Notice that there are several instances of harp harmonics in this study piece. The harmonics in bars four and five are natural, based on open strings, and executed entirely with the right hand, as explained in Example 5a.

Example 7j

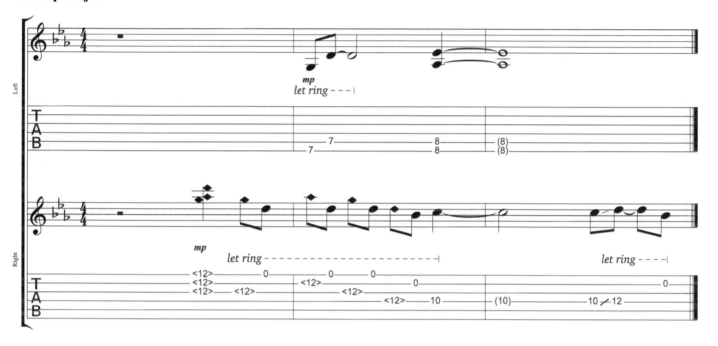

Example 7k shows how the next section builds by adding a percussive hit on beat 3 with the left hand.

Bar thirty-two involves simultaneously hammering on with the barred inverted index finger to the 7th fret and playing a tapped harmonic on the 12th fret with the right hand.

The strummed chord that follows (indicated with a vertical wavy line) is played by barring the first finger on the 8th fret, and strumming all of the strings with the right hand (including the open strings).

Example 7k

The opening chord of Example 7l is played by barring the fourth finger of the inverted left hand across the third fret, placing the index finger on the fourth string, then strumming with the right hand (hence the empty right-hand stave at this point).

Allow the right hand fingers to unfold when picking in order to arpeggiate the chord.

Next pick the open fourth string with the second finger, fret the chord that follows with the inverted left hand (using the fourth and first fingers) and pick with the right hand thumb and first finger.

Example 7l

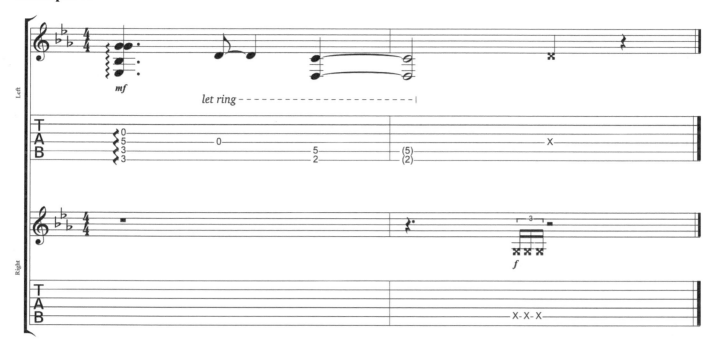

The Coda features lots of right hand strumming so the right hand stave is largely empty for these sections.

Example 7m

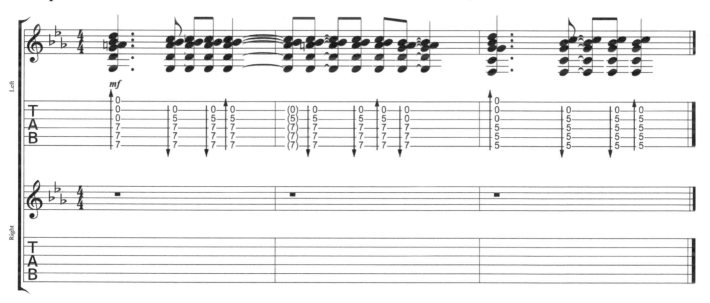

The only remaining part of the piece that requires some clarification is the strumming interspersed with fast triplets in the Coda.

Barre the left hand first finger in the inverted position on the 7th fret, then hammer the fourth finger onto the 5th fret. The 12th fret note that follows is tapped with the right hand. I have notated this whole lick in the right hand stave to make it easier to read, but it definitely needs to be played with both hands.

Example 7n

Boquete

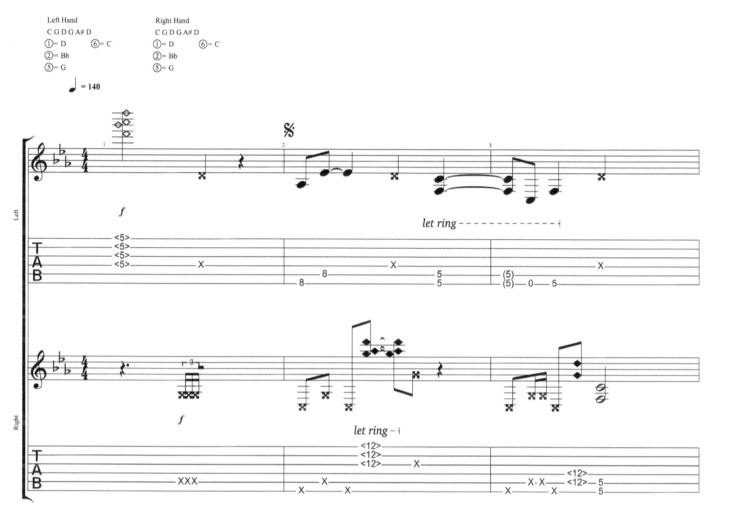

(Harp harmonic effect picked with right hand, chord shape fretted with left)

Chapter 8. Solo Fingerstyle Arranging

We have focused in detail on many of the challenging modern fingerstyle techniques, and worked through studies for each one. Now we will take a brief look at possibly the most intriguing and useful aspect of this style: being able to construct your own solo arrangements.

This is a huge topic that would warrant a book in its own right, so I can't do it justice here. However, I do want to pass on some tips that will serve as a launch pad for your own explorations.

I've taken the familiar folk song *Danny Boy* to demonstrate how you might take a simple tune and begin to develop a modern fingerstyle arrangement.

You can watch the videos of the full performance piece and all of the examples in this chapter here: **http://geni.us/acousticvids**

Example 8a is played in standard tuning.

Example 8a

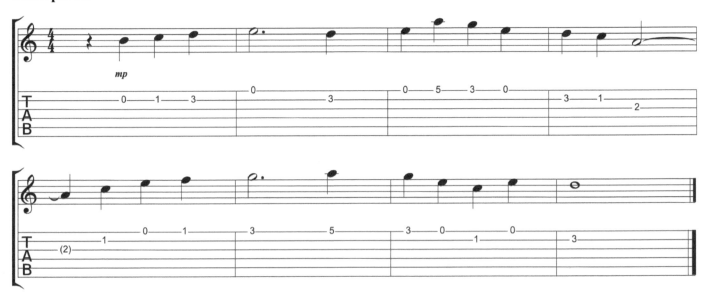

Next, we need some harmony to accompany the melody. This simplest way to achieve this is to add sustained chords on the lower strings, with the melody on the high strings, to create a simple chord-melody arrangement.

Example 8b

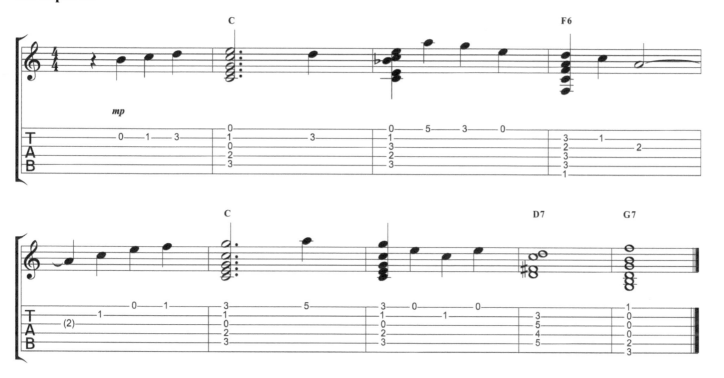

You will probably find the chords fairly basic and a bit uninspiring. Plus, they don't sustain well with the melody because they get in each other's way. It's messy and not very well considered.

So, what are our options? Here are a few arranging strategies. We can…

- Change the octave of the melody or chords, so that they don't interfere with each other so much

- Change the key to make better use of open strings for bass notes, or natural harmonics for melody notes, for example

- Change the tuning of the guitar to open up more options (for example to allow a low C bass note)

- Any combination of the above

I tend to always do at least one of the above, but first I want to alter the chords, adding in some substitutions that will make the harmony more musical. I will stay in standard tuning for this, to make it easier to see what is happening.

In Example 8c I have now…

- Added a descending chromatic line in the C Major harmony to create more interest (C, Cmaj7, C7)

- Harmonised some of the melody in 6ths

- Used "back cycling" (the technique of back-tracking through the Circle of Fifths in order to re-harmonise an otherwise static and uninteresting harmony). This way we still arrive at the desired destination (D7), but the journey is more interesting

- I have also changed the fingerings (for example in bar one) to allow the notes to ring together, and added an embellishment in the penultimate bar

Example 8c

Having got this far, I'm now going move to an alternate tuning – in this case DADGAD. I have transposed the arrangement to D Major to make the most of the open strings and natural harmonics in DADGAD tuning. I have also added a few embellishments that DADGAD tuning makes possible.

Retune your guitar now and check it out.

Example 8d (DADGAD tuning)

Now take a look at the whole arrangement.

Be careful with the unusual "strummed" harmonic in the final bar. You will need to place the right hand index finger over the 16th fret while maintaining the 4th fret bar with your left hand. Use your right hand, third fingernail to pick the strings. Drag both fingers parallel to each other from the high to low strings to achieve the effect.

Danny Boy

Conclusion

"Modern fingerstyle acoustic guitar" is an expansive musical genre and demands a wide range of techniques. In this book, my aim has been to equip you with the *essential* techniques and give you an insight into how to execute them cleanly. Many of these techniques take a long time to perfect, so don't worry if you feel your progress is slow.

As well as the examples I've included, I hope that the study pieces themselves help you to develop the disciplines of modern fingerstyle guitar – as well as being enjoyable performance pieces in their own right.

Remember, if you get stuck on one particular technique, to take it slowly and break it down into smaller parts. This will invariably help you to solve any problems and master the technique.

Above all, enjoy the journey and never stop learning new things.

Have fun!

Daryl.

Made in United States
Troutdale, OR
07/07/2023

11036083R00064